THOMAS HARDY

THOMAS HARDY

For Conan Cook

Cornelia Cook

Life and Works

Jane Austen
The Brontës
Thomas Hardy
Hemingway
D.H. Lawrence
Katherine Mansfield
George Orwell
Shakespeare
H.G. Wells
Virginia Woolf

Note: Quotations are from *The Life and Work of Thomas Hardy* (ed. M. Millgate), which is a new edition of the *Early Life* and *Later Years* by Florence Hardy.

Cover illustration by David Armitage

First published in 1989 by
Wayland (Publishers) Ltd
61 Western Road, Hove
East Sussex BN3 1JD, England

© Copyright 1989 Wayland (Publishers) Ltd

Series adviser: Dr Cornelia Cook
Series designer: David Armitage
Series editor: Susannah Foreman

British Library Cataloguing in Publication Data
Cook, Cornelia
    Thomas Hardy. — (Life and works)
    1. Fiction in English. Hardy Thomas,
    1840-1928 - Critical studies
    1. Title
    823'.8

    ISBN 1-85210-420-1

Typeset by Kalligraphics Ltd, Horley, Surrey
Printed in Italy by G. Canale & C.S.p.A., Turin
Bound in the UK by Mac Lehose & Partners, Portsmouth

Contents

1 Life and Early Works

June 2, 1840. It was in a lonely and silent spot between woodland and heathland that Thomas Hardy was born, about eight o'clock on Tuesday morning the 2nd of June, 1840, the place of his birth being the seven-roomed rambling house that stands easternmost of the few scattered dwellings called Higher Bockhampton, in the parish of Stinsford, Dorset. The domiciles were quaint, brass-knockered, and green-shuttered then, some with green garden-doors and white balls on the posts, and mainly occupied by lifeholders of substantial footing like the Hardys themselves.

That is from the first paragraph of *The Life of Thomas Hardy* by Florence Emily Hardy, the poet's second wife. But a second look at those two sentences would tell the reader familiar with Hardy's works that the writing was his. And indeed, *The Life of Thomas Hardy* is not biography, but autobiography. It was an ingenious scheme devised in his old age by Hardy, who had always been concerned to protect his private life from public scrutiny. He wrote his memoirs – revealing precisely what he wished to have known and concealing much – as if from his wife's point of view. 'My idea, of course,' he said 'is to have the work appear after my death as a biography of myself written by my wife.'

The writing in the passage is characteristically Hardy's in its content and its style. 'It was in a lonely and silent spot

Opposite Thomas Hardy at age 32. In this year Hardy gave up architecture for a writing career.

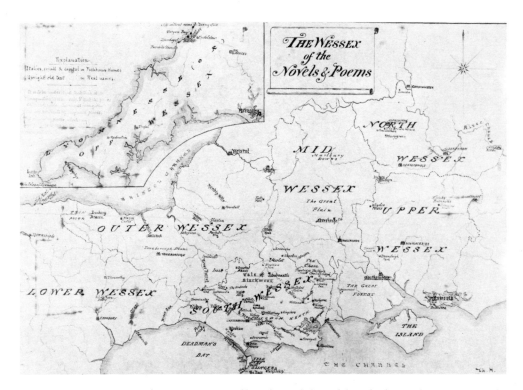

The Wessex
of the
Novels & Poems

Explanation.
Italics, small & capital — Fictitious Names
Upright old text — Real names.

Hardy's map of his fictional Wessex. He explained 'It is to be understood that this is an imaginary Wessex only.'

Opposite *Hardy's drawing of his birthplace at Higher Bockhampton, the cottage described in 'Domicilium'.*

between woodland and heathland that Thomas Hardy was born.' The spot is in Dorset, in the heart of the south middle and western part of England for which Hardy was to resurrect the ancient name of 'Wessex', and which was to become the 'circumscribed scene' of his fictions. The spot, 'lonely and silent', is like the man as he liked to present himself once he had become famous. And its location 'between woodland and heathland' recalls the landscapes that dominate some of his best known novels and recur in his poetry.

Hardy calls attention to the 'seven-roomed rambling house' and its precise relation to the 'few scattered dwellings' of Higher Bockhampton with the same exactness that the one-time architect describes the dwellings and surroundings of his fictional characters. And then he goes on, with a characteristic particularity of visual description, to notice the brass knockers, the green shutters and doors, and 'white balls on the posts' of the houses where decoration and architectural features announce the class and character of the people who live in them. Social class was always important to Hardy: so

A Dorset village band. The Hardys 'were considered among the best church-players in the neighbourhood.'

much so that he elevated that of his ancestors in his biography and made class a significant theme in all his fictions.

Hardy had written a poem about the house at Higher Bockhampton when he was seventeen. He called the poem 'Domicilium'. That, too, seems to be recalled in the description where the words 'the domiciles were quaint' themselves derive a quaintness from the use of the un-homely noun 'domiciles'. It is characteristic that in the passage the interest is displaced from the subject of the biography, Hardy himself, on to the place, the community and the family. It is characteristic because while revealing these details it *conceals* Hardy the man as effectively as do the many works of fiction and poetry which exploit his

most intimate experiences and yet absolutely resist
becoming 'confessional' or 'autobiographical' literature.

Thomas Hardy's father came from a family whose men
had for several generations been stone-masons; the senior
Thomas Hardy was a successful builder or master-mason.
The Hardys 'became well-known as violinists' and 'were
considered among the best church-players in the
neighbourhood'; according to Hardy, they were
handsome men who 'danced hornpipes, jigs and other
folk-dances' with skill and enthusiasm. Hardy's
grandmother, Mary Hardy, fed the future novelist's love
of narrative and his store of folk and family history with
her vivid memories and lively stories. Hardy celebrated
her in the poem 'One We Knew'.

She showed us the spot where the maypole was yearly
      planted,
   And where the bandsman stood
While breeched and kerchiefed partners whirled, and
      panted
   To choose each other for good.

She told of that far-back day when they learnt
      astounded
   Of the death of the King of France:
Of the Terror; and then of Bonaparte's unbounded
   Ambition and arrogance.
        . . .
With cap-framed face and long gaze into the embers –
   We seated around her knees –
She would dwell on such dead themes, not as one who
      remembers,
   But rather as one who sees.

She seemed one left behind of a band gone distant
   So far that no tongue could hail:
Past things retold were to her as things existent,
   Things present but as a tale.

Hardy's mother, the former Jemima Hand, was a youthful, strong-minded woman who, though of very humble origins, was a great reader. She, too, had a stock of folklore and legends, and her son remembered her singing the popular songs of the day. One of Hardy's biographers says that Mrs Hardy handed on to her son 'vivid independence, a lively sense of humour, and a sombre view of fate'. These seeming contradictions became part of the richness of Hardy's experience, and are reflected in the varied tones of his novels and poems. Mrs Hardy, the model for Mrs Yeobright in *The Return of the Native*, was ambitious for her family, especially for her eldest son Thomas; he and her other children, Mary, Henry and Katherine, all remained close to her throughout her long life.

Pictures from Hardy's childhood are to be found throughout his novels in glimpses of old rural customs, in the landscapes of Dorset, its villages and market towns and its vestiges of pre-Roman and Roman habitations, and in the precise descriptions of nature which Hardy called 'part of the country boy's life'. Hardy celebrated the

Opposite *Jemima Hardy, Thomas Hardy's mother.*

traditional rural life that was fast dying out of such hamlets as Higher Bockhampton in *Under the Greenwood Tree*. But the best picture of the child Thomas at home with his parents is his own lyric 'The Self-Unseeing'.

Here is the ancient floor,
Footworn and hollowed and thin,
Here was the former door
 Where the dead feet walked in.

She sat here in her chair,
Smiling into the fire;
He who played stood there,
Bowing it higher and higher.

Childlike, I danced in a dream;
Blessings emblazoned that day;
Everything glowed with a gleam;
Yet we were looking away!

Hardy's cottage:
'Here is the ancient
floor, footworn and
hollowed and thin...'

The poem is typical of Hardy in that it looks back to the past, and starts from a view of a place. A return to the old place evokes a moment from the past; the blessedness which exists in the pure unselfconsciousness of that moment *depends* on that carelessness of the moment, and it necessarily co-exists in the poem with the present awareness of loss.

Hardy was an observant boy. He noticed keenly the ordinary and extraordinary features of his surroundings. He notes among his early memories: 'men in stocks, corn-law agitations, mail-coaches, road-waggons, tinder-boxes, and candle-snuffing'. The ordinary things he noticed become the stuff of a marvellous realism in his fictions. The 'four grey silk flounces' of an early Victorian lady's dress re-emerge in a story written forty years later. The extraordinary things he observed become striking episodes or shaping forces in his fiction. As an adolescent Hardy witnessed two hangings. One was of a woman. The second Hardy watched from a hill on the heath outside Dorchester, through a telescope. The scene was in summer sunshine and Hardy saw justice done - 'the white figure dropped downwards' - as 'the town clock struck eight'. These experiences became the fatality towards which the whole of *Tess of the d'Urbervilles* tends. In the concluding

Dorchester, Hardy's 'Casterbridge', was the county town, centre of local government and meeting-place of the county court. It was a busy market town, with a military garrison.

scene of the novel Tess's husband and sister walk away from 'Wintoncester' on the morning of Tess's hanging.

When they had nearly reached the top of the great West Hill the clocks in the town struck eight . . . impelled by a force that seemed to overrule their will, [they] suddenly stood still, turned, and waited . . .

The prospect from this summit was almost unlimited . . . landscape beyond landscape, till the horizon was lost in the radiance of the sun hanging above it.

Against these far stretches of country rose, in front of the other city edifices, a large red-brick building . . . From the middle of the building an ugly flat-topped octagonal tower ascended against the east horizon, and viewed from this spot, on its shady side and against the light, it seemed the one blot on the city's beauty. Yet it was with this blot, and not with the beauty, that the two gazers were concerned.

Upon the cornice of the tower a tall staff was fixed. Their eyes were riveted on it. A few minutes after the hour had struck something moved slowly up the staff, and extended itself upon the breeze. It was a black flag.

Thatched village houses: Puddletown, Dorset. A number of Hardy's ancestors came from Puddletown and he frequently visited his cousins there.

The scene in the novel is a conflation and re-presentation of Hardy's own experiences. But the novelist heightens its tension and impact. The 'gazers' are '*impelled*' to turn. A survey of the scene from their hill, in which Hardy supplies every detail of landscape and buildings in view, holding us in suspense, and drawing us slowly, through the gradual focussing of vision on the prison and tower, leads us to the moment of understanding – of what *has happened*. Indeed it was over at the outset, when the clock chimed eight. The black flag rises, as if by its own agency: signal and symbol of the judicial murder which Hardy ironically calls 'justice', and which here gains its disturbing impact from the fact that it is *not* described.

In 1848 Hardy was sent to the village school at Bockhampton. The school had been founded by the lady of the manor, Mrs Julia Augusta Martin of Kingston Maurward, a childless woman who was especially fond of the young Thomas Hardy and who was for him an object of admiration and boyish love. At this well-run school he 'excelled' at arithmetic and geography, though he confessed 'his handwriting was indifferent'. The following year he was sent further afield, to the county town of Dorchester to attend the British School, a

Opposite *Hardy at 19. While working for John Hicks, architect and church-restorer in Dorchester, Hardy studied the Greek and Latin classics, doing his reading between five and eight in the morning.*

18

Michaelmas market, Dorchester.

Nonconformist school where the headmaster was 'a good teacher of Latin' and Hardy was soon introduced to the old Eton grammar. When this master established his own independent 'commercial academy' for able students in 1853 Hardy continued to walk from quiet rural Bockhampton to busy Dorchester, where the communications revolution brought about by the railways and telegraph brought the news and the popular songs of London to the ears of the boy who was advancing in his knowledge of classics and technical subjects.

Hardy's schooldays were a mixture of avid study and strenuous fun; he played the violin at village functions and attended entertainments in Dorchester. He fell in love repeatedly, too – once at Bockhampton school, later with a gamekeeper's red-haired daughter whom he wrote about years later in the poem 'To Lizbie Browne,'

Sweet Lizbie Browne
How you could smile,
How you could sing! -
How archly wile
In glance-giving,
Sweet Lizbie Browne!

'I let you slip;/Shaped not a sign' he says of Lizbie, and in his next infatuation, too, shyness prevented him from declaring his love. Louisa Harding, a well-to-do farmer's daughter, captured Hardy's devotion and is remembered in a number of his later poems ('The Passer-by', 'Louie', 'To Louisa in the Lane'). 'He used to pass, well-trimmed and brushed,/ My window every day', the poet has Louisa recall, 'And when I smiled on him he blushed,/ That youth, quite as a girl might; aye,/ In the shyest way'. In the *Life* Hardy recalls meeting Louisa in the lane, but being too bashful to speak more than 'a murmured "Good evening", while poor Louisa had no word to say'. 'That "Good evening",'he concludes, 'was the only word that passed between them.' Throughout his life Hardy was susceptible to young women's charms; he fell in love imaginatively, flirtatiously and platonically over and over again. He made this tendency to become infatuated with an idealized woman the subject of a poem, 'The Well-Beloved'.

-O faultless is her dainty form,
  And luminous her mind;
She is the God-created norm
  Of perfect womankind!

'I am thy very dream', the apparition tells the poet. Hardy's last published novel, *The Well-Beloved*, tells the story of an artist who pursues this 'very dream' in a succession of women from his youth to his old age.

At the age of sixteen Hardy left school. Limited funds and his insufficient academic preparation placed university admission out of his reach, but he determined to continue to gain for himself a classical education while pursuing a professional career. His abilities were noticed and he was offered an apprenticeship to Mr John Hicks, an architect and church-restorer in Dorchester. Under Hicks Hardy worked at the 'restoration' of Gothic churches. Gothic is the style of architecture which dominated in Western Europe from the twelfth century to the sixteenth. The most notable characteristic of Gothic architecture is the pointed arch, used in the structure of buildings and in their decoration. Along with the pointed arch, features of the Gothic style include vaulted roofs, flying buttresses and grotesque sculptures. John Ruskin in his essay 'The Nature of Gothic' (1853) noted that the Gothic style combined a 'tendency to delight in fantastic and ludicrous images' with 'a love of fact' expressed in forms taken from familiar 'nature'.

St. George's Chapel, Windsor. An example of fifteenth-century Gothic. The staircase is Victorian.

Buildings which soared upward in 'faith and aspiration' still reflected the shapes of the foliage of earth and incorporated the humour and individuality of their builders in gargoyles and exuberant ornament. Ruskin's description of Gothic ornament reflects these varied elements:

St. Peter's Church, Dorchester. Hardy was assigned by Hicks to draw a ground plan of St. Peter's which was undergoing 'improvements' under Hick's direction.

. . . the Gothic ornament stands out in prickly independence, and frostly fortitude, jutting into crockets, and freezing into pinnacles; here starting up into a monster, there germinating into a blossom, anon knitting

23

itself into a branch, alternately thorny, bossy, and bristly, or writhed into every form of nervous entanglement; but even when most graceful, never for an instant languid, always quickest; erring, if at all, ever on the side of brusquerie.

(*The Stones of Venice* Vol II, Ch.6)

Hardys work taught him to love especially the late medieval 'perpendicular' style with its distinctive vertical lines, which he celebrated in the poem 'The Abbey Mason', '. . . The ogee arches transom-topped, / The tracery-stalks by spandrels stopped, / Petrified lacework – lightly lined / On ancient massiveness behind – . . . '. His work involved measuring and drawing – the work he describes his young architect-hero engaged in in the opening of *A Laodicean*.

. . . the sketcher still lingered at his occupation of measuring and copying the chevroned doorway, a bold and quaint example of a transitional style of architecture, which formed the tower entrance to an English village church.

. . .

He took his measurements carefully, and as if he reverenced the old workers whose trick he was endeavouring to aquire six hundred years after the original performance had ceased and the performers passed into the unseen. By means of a strip of lead called a leaden tape, which he pressed around and into the fillets and hollows with his finger and thumb, he transferred the exact contour of each moulding to his drawing, that lay on the sketching-stool a few feet distant; where was also a sketching-block, a small T-square, a bow-pencil, and other mathematical instruments. When he had marked down the line thus fixed, he returned to the doorway to copy another as before.

In addition to learning the trade, Hardy kept up his academic studies. Hicks encouraged Hardy and a fellow-pupil in their reading of Latin and Greek, and when difficult questions arose, they consulted William Barnes, the Dorset dialect poet who was an expert philologist and grammarian and who, conveniently, taught school next door.

In 1862 Hardy took a major step, moving to London where he found employment with the architect Arthur

Blomfield. The London experience was intense: his intellectual life was enlivened, his cultural experience broadened, his health endangered, and the major changes in his career prepared for. Hardy again worked at restoring and designing churches. He read widely – in Shakespeare, the English Romantic poets, in Positivist philosophers and the great English Victorian thinkers J. S. Mill, J. H. Newman, and probably Charles Darwin. He attended the theatre frequently. He also began to write poetry, essays and novels. When he returned to Dorset in 1867, again to work for Hicks and to recover his health, Hardy's plans had taken a new direction. He had given up any remaining idea of aspiring to university or to the Church; indeed, he recognized that – while entertaining great affection for the rituals of the Church, the music, the language of liturgy and Scripture, for church buildings, and for the religious impulse itself – he could not be an orthodox believer. His interest in architecture as a profession waned and the attractiveness of a literary career grew.

The first of Hardy's novels, written in 1867-1868, was called *The Poor Man and the Lady*. It was never published because, although several publishers thought it not bad, none thought it good enough for them – or Hardy – to risk the costs of publication. It had too much of youthful hotheadedness about it. Hardy was not pleased with this response and he destroyed the novel – but he described it in the *Life* as:

> a sweeping dramatic satire of the squirearchy and nobility, London society, the vulgarity of the middle class, modern Christianity, church-restoration, and political and domestic morals in general, the author's views, in fact, being obviously those of a young man with a passion for reforming the world – those of many a young man before and after him; the tendency of the writing being socialistic, not to say revolutionary . . .
>
> (p. 61)

Opposite *Letter from Macmillan and Co. rejecting* The Poor Man and the Lady.

This aspect repelled Alexander Macmillan of the Macmillan firm while for his reader John Morley, the 'rawness of absurdity', making the book 'like some clever lad's dream', spoilt the promise of much 'strong and fresh' writing.

Thomas Hardy Esqre
    Bockhampton
Dorchester.

MACMILLAN AND CO.

PUBLISHERS TO THE UNIVERSITY OF OXFORD,

16, BEDFORD STREET, COVENT GARDEN, W.C.

Dear Sir,   London, Aug. 10. 1868.

I have read through the novel you
were so good as send me, with care & with
much interest and admiration, but feeling at
the same time that it has what seem to me
(fatal) drawbacks to its success, and, what I
think from the book itself you would feel even
more strongly, to its truthfulness & justice.
Your delineation of county life among working
men is admirable, and though I can only judge
of it from the corresponding life in Scotland, which
I know well when young, palpably truthful. Your
pictures of character among Londoners and especially
the upper classes are sharp clear incisive and in
many respects true, but they are wholly dark,
not a ray of light visible to relieve the darkness &
therefore exaggerated & untrue in their result. Their
frivolity heartlessness, selfishness are great & terrible,
but there are other sides, and I can hardly conceive
that they would do otherwise than what you
seek to avoid: "throw down the volume in disgust."
Even the worst of them would hardly I think do
things that you describe them as doing. For instance:.
Is it conceivable that any man however base &
soul corrupted would do as you make the Hon Fog
allamont do at the close, accept an estimate for
his daughters tomb - because it cost him nothing?
He had already so far broken through the prejudices
of his class as to send for Strong in the hope of saving his
daughters life. Then is it at all possible that a
public body would in public retract their award
on the grounds you make them avow in the
case of the Palace of Hobbies Company?

~~The Mellstock Quire~~

or

Under the Greenwood Tree

A rural painting of the Dutch School.

Part I. Winter.

Chapter I

Mellstock Lane.

To dwellers in a wood, almost every species of
tree has its voice as well as its feature. At the
passing of the breeze the fir-trees sob & moan no less
distinctly than they rock: the holly whistles as it battles
with itself: the ash hisses amid its quivering: the
beech rustles as its flat boughs rise & fall. And winter,
which modifies the notes of such trees as shed their leaves,
does not destroy their individuality.

On a cold & starry Christmas-eve, not less than a
generation ago a man was passing along a lane in
the darkness of a plantation that whispered thus
distinctively to his intelligence. All the evidences of his
nature were those afforded by the spirit of his footsteps,
which succeeded each other lightly & quickly, & by
the liveliness of his voice as he sang in a rural
cadence.
            " — With the rose & the lily
            And the daffodowndilly,
      The lads & the lasses a-sheep-shearing go."

The novelist George Meredith was the publisher's reader who turned the novel down at Chapman and Hall, and he advised Hardy to set about a new novel with less rant and more plot. Hardy certainly took him seriously: *Desperate Remedies* which followed, published in 1871, is a sensational, melodramatic novel with a plot that even the characters seem to have difficulty negotiating. The firm of Messrs Tinsley published this book (with Hardy, who had to guarantee the printing costs, taking most of the risk). Tinsley wanted Hardy's next book, too, and when Hardy explained that he had not come off very well financially with *Desperate Remedies*, Tinsley said, "Pon my soul, Mr. Hardy, you wouldn't have got another man in London to print it! Oh, be hanged if you would! 'twas a blood-curdling story! Now please try to find that new manuscript and let me see it.' (*Life*, p.88).

The new book was *Under the Greenwood Tree*. It was originally to be called 'The Mellstock Quire', and it combines a commemoration of the village church musicians of 'fifty or sixty years' earlier with a happy story of young love. Hardy had noted that sections of *The Poor*

Opposite *Hardy's manuscript of the opening of* Under the Greenwood Tree, *originally titled 'The Mellstock Quire'.*

Victorian church musicians (Langton Matravers orchestra).

Man and the Lady portraying rural characters and customs had won praise from the publishers' readers. So he had set about exploiting those elements in a pastoral story on the model of a romantic comedy. Pastoral is an ancient genre in which the lives and loves of shepherds and other rural figures are idealized and celebrated. English writers from Spenser to Milton and Marvell and Pope had written pastoral poetry. Shakespeare had incorporated elements of pastoral in his romantic comedies and later romances. Rural or woodland settings, communities of shepherds or foresters in those works provided locations of escape where the confusions and wrongs of the worlds of court or city could be resolved or redressed. *Under the Greenwood Tree* is the title of a song in *As You Like It*, and just as escape to the Forest of Arden in Shakespeare's comedy permits error to be corrected, danger to be kept at bay, and young love to flourish, so in the novel the rural village community provides a scene where change and continuity accommodate each other. Against nature's seasonal cycle are depicted the romance of Dick Dewy and Fancy Day and the disbanding of the Mellstock church choir with its traditional instrumentalists and singers in favour of an organ and a single organist. The novel is in five parts, like the acts of a comedy, beginning with 'Winter', and progressing through 'Spring', 'Summer' and 'Autumn' to

Opposite Dick Dewy, from an engraving in one of the first editions of the novel.

Hardy's cottage: model for the scene of Tranter Dewy's dance (Under the Greenwood Tree).

the successful 'Conclusion', in which Fancy and Dick are married as another midsummer returns:

> ... just subsequent to that point in the development of the seasons when country people go to bed among nearly naked trees, are lulled to sleep by a fall of rain, and awake next morning among green ones; when the landscape appears embarrassed with the sudden weight and brilliancy of its leaves; when the night-jar comes and strikes up for the summer his tune of one note ... and when cuckoos, blackbirds, and sparrows, that have hitherto been merry and respectful neighbours, become noisy and persistent intimates.
>
> (Part 5, ch.1)

Thomas Leaf: 'He's rather silly by nature and never could get fat; though he's a' excellent treble, and so we keep him on' (Under the Greenwood Tree).

The members of the Mellstock choir are comical rustics, of a more literary than realistic kind; they recall the 'rude mechanicals' of *A Midsummer Night's Dream*, and like Shakespeare's troupe they provide a plot which parallels and interacts with the lovers' story. But the Dewy household, where three generations jostle against each other and a fourth is prepared for, is the centre of a picture of village life, showing the interactions within and between families and social groups.

Under the Greenwood Tree is subtitled 'A Rural Painting of the Dutch School'. Presenting a single self-contained community in the relatively short space of a year and a half, the novel has the homely unity of a Dutch painting. George Eliot, too, had likened her novels to Dutch paintings in their realism and their concern for ordinary people in local or domestic circumstances. This realism – seen in descriptions of the interior of homes (the Dewys', the Days'), of occupations, and of traditional customs and entertainments – enlivens the conventional form of the pastoral comedy in *Under the Greenwood Tree*.

'Mellstock' Church: St. Michael's, Stinsford, near Dorchester.

Opposite *Hardy's architectural sketch for the restoration of the church at St. Juliot.*

Hardy's enthusiasm for the simple love story of Dick and Fancy may have reflected his own mood, for in 1870 he had fallen in love with Emma Lavinia Gifford. He met her when sent to work on the restoration of an old church at St. Juliot in Cornwall. Emma was the rector's sister-in-law, and she seems rapidly to have determined that the Architect, as she called Hardy in a memoir she wrote of the time, was to be her husband. Hardy's poem 'When I Set Out for Lyonnesse' commemorates that trip to Cornwall and its momentousness.

> What would bechance at Lyonnesse
> While I should sojourn there
> No prophet durst declare,
>   . . .
> When I came back from Lyonnesse
> With magic in my eyes,
> All marked with mute surmise
> My radiance rare and fathomless,
> When I came back from Lyonnesse
> With magic in my eyes!

Emma Gifford at St. Juliot rectory.

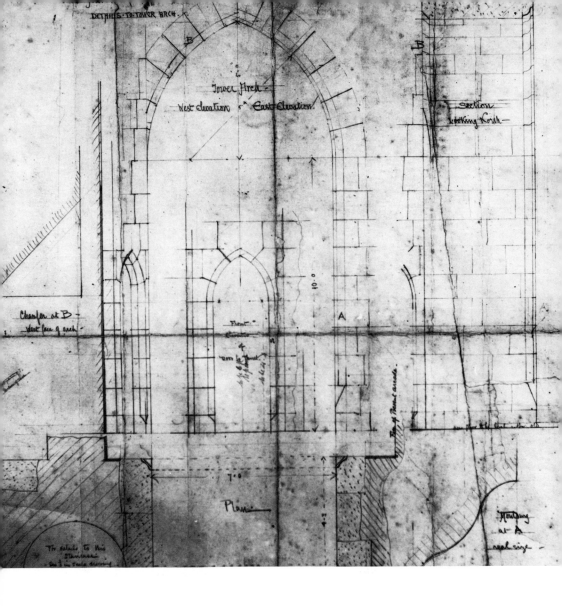

The Architect returned repeatedly to St. Juliot, to the church and to visit Emma. She recalled,

I rode my pretty mare Fanny and he walked by my side, and I showed him some [more] of the neighbourhood – the cliffs, along the roads, and through the scattered hamlets, sometimes gazing down at the solemn small shores below, where the seals lived, coming out of great deep caverns very occasionally. We sketched and talked of books . . .

(*Life*, p.71)

These visits, she reports, 'merged in those of further acquaintance and affection, to end in marriage, but not till after four years'. Hardy admired Emma for her vitality ('She was so *living*, he used to say'), her gracefulness, and 'her corn-coloured hair abundant in its coils'. He based 'the character and appearance' of Elfride Swancourt, the heroine of *A Pair of Blue Eyes* (published in 1873) on Emma 'in quite young womanhood'. Those visits, the Cornish landscape of their courting, and the particulars of Emma's dress and person at that time are the details which 'haunt' Hardy many years later in the magnificent series of poems he wrote after Emma's death, in November 1912.

> O the opal and the sapphire of that wandering western
>   sea,
> And the woman riding high above with bright hair
>   flapping free –
> The woman whom I loved so, and who loyally loved
>   me.
>
> ('Beeny Cliff')

> . . . Let me view you, then,
> Standing as when I drew near to the town
> Where you would wait for me: yes, as I knew you then,
> Even to the original air-blue gown!
>
> ('The Voice')

> Facing round about me everywhere,
>   With your nut- coloured hair,
> And gray eyes, and rose-flush coming and going.
> I see what you are doing: you are leading me on
>   To the spots we knew when we haunted here together,
> The waterfall, above which the mist-bow shone
>   At the then fair hour in the then fair weather,
> And the cave just under, with a voice still so hollow
>   That it seems to call out to me from forty years ago . . .
>
> ('After a Journey')

The last words of *Under the Greenwood Tree* are Fancy's on her wedding night, 'O, 'tis the nightingale'. They nearly echo Juliet's 'It was the nightingale', on her tragic wedding night in Shakespeare's *Romeo and Juliet* as the lovers turn from their private world to confront fatal reality, and they remind us that the idyll of young love is unlikely to last. Indeed, Dick has earlier noted this peculiarity in older

Beeny Cliff
(March 1870 — March 1913)

I.

O the opal and the sapphire of that wandering western sea,
And the woman riding high above with bright hair flapping free —
The woman whom I loved so, and who loyally loved me.

II.

The ~~white mews~~ puffins plained below us, and the waves seemed far away
In a nether sky, engrossed in saying their endless babbling say,
As we laughed lightheartedly aloft on that clear-sunned March day.

III

A little cloud then cloaked us, and there flew an irised rain,
And the Atlantic dyed its levels with a dull misfeatured stain,
And then the sun burst out ~~anew~~ again, and purples prinked the main.

IV.

— Still in all its chasmal beauty bulks old Beeny to the sky,
And shall she and I not go there once again now March is nigh,
And the sweet things said in that March say anew there by and by?

V.

What if ~~Nay. Though~~ still in chasmal beauty looms that wild weird western shore,
The woman now is — elsewhere — whom the ambling pony bore,
And nor knows nor cares for Beeny, and will see it nevermore.

married couples: 'Dick wondered how it was that when people were married they could be so blind to romance . . . so dreadfully practical and undemonstrative of the Passion as his father and mother were.'

Hardy and Emma's forty years of marriage were not altogether happy. As the poet phrases it in 'After a Journey', 'Summer gave us sweets, but autumn wrought

Manuscript of 'Beeny Cliff' ('Poems of 1912-13').

division' and 'Things were not lastly as firstly well/With us twain . . . ', but compromises and contrived distance kept them together, and Hardy recognized in his grief the irony that mortal life does not live up to the magic of anticipation, nor can it recapture the uncomplicated intensity of remembered 'joy'.

In his next novel, *A Pair of Blue Eyes*, Hardy used the forms of romance – a young girl has two suitors who (unbeknownst to each other) vie for her hand, and ultimately she marries a third, a lord. But the novel is not, after all, a typical romance. The first young man, honest and worthy but of humble origins, goes abroad to advance his career so that he may marry Elfride. In his absence, her affections transfer themselves to his older friend, now rival, aptly called Knight. But just as Elfride is not the impeccable lady of romance, Knight is not the chivalric hero. Rather he is self-centred, self-important, and prudish to the extent that, learning that Elfride has appeared in a compromising situation with another, he permits her no defence, and will not forgive her. He abandons her to unhappiness, a loveless marriage and death. Romance follows a conventional pattern, based on unfailing virtues of courage, constancy and service. Hardy's novel shows that humans are victims of the instability of their own emotions and the limitedness of their understanding. The emotion of one moment often does not survive altered circumstances. When one person idealizes or idolizes another, he or she fails to see the real person, and may overlook genuine virtues or exaggerate the failings which appear when real and ideal clash. Knight, who expects perfection of Elfride, is a precursor of Angel Clare in *Tess of the d'Urbervilles*. Like Angel, he understands the mistakes of a narrow, self-centred judgement too late.

The pastoral that was reflected in rural settings in *Desperate Remedies* and which Hardy called attention to in *Under the Greenwood Tree* remained an important element in his works. Nature has a life of its own in Hardy's poems and novels:

To dwellers in a wood almost every species of tree has its voice as well as its feature. At the passing of the breeze the fir-trees sob and moan no less distinctly than they rock; the

Opposite *Emma Hardy in maturity.*

holly whistles as it battles with itself; the ash hisses amid its quiverings; the beech rustles while its flat boughs rise and fall. And winter, which modifies the note of such trees as shed their leaves, does not destroy its individuality.

(*Under the Greenwood Tree*, Part 1, ch. 1)

But nature also frequently becomes a means of examining and commenting on *human* nature. *In A Pair of Blue Eyes* Knight is forced to acknowledge his own unimportance when confronted with nature's power, magnitude and duration. He finds himself stranded on the side of a cliff over a threatening ocean with the geological accretions of

Opposite *Creech Barrow, an ancient burial site near Church Knowle, Isle of Purbeck.*

Tess's Return:
' "Well! - my dear Tess!" exclaimed her surprised mother ... "Have you come home to be married?" "No. I have not come for that, mother." '

eons registered in the rocks which stare him in the face. *In Far from the Madding Crowd* nature's broad continuities expose human misjudgements, while nature's fatalities match the tragic substance of human lives. In *The Return of the Native* nature acquires a life of its own and a power to shape human lives: Egdon Heath represents fate itself – inescapable and formative.

Nature could become an image for an idea in Hardy. The song of 'The Darkling Thrush' becomes for the poet the note of 'some blessed Hope whereof he knew / And I was unaware'. Nature could usefully expose and demonstrate the subjectivity of humans. In a poem called 'The Milkmaid' Hardy mocks the preconceptions formed from pastoral poetry. In keeping with them, the poet idealizes and entirely mis-reads his pastoral 'Phyllis'.

> Under a daised bank
> There stands a rich red ruminating cow,
>   And hard against her flank
> A cotton-hooded milkmaid bends her brow.
>
>   The flowery river-ooze
> Upheaves and falls; the milk purrs in the pail;
>   Few pilgrims but would choose
> The peace of such a life in such a vale.
>
>   The maid breathes words – to vent,
> It seems, her sense of Nature's scenery,
>   Of whose life, sentiment,
> And essence, very part itself is she.

He thinks she is content with life and in harmony with nature, and possibly distressed by the un-pastoral sound of a passing train. But no: she is thinking of a fickle lover and a new dress from the city:

>   Nay! Phyllis does not dwell
> On visual and familiar things like these;
>
>   What moves her is the spell
> Of inner themes and inner poetries:
>
>   Could but by Sunday morn
> Her gay new gown come, meads might dry to dun,
>   Trains shriek till ears were torn,
> If Fred would not prefer that Other One.

43

While laughing at *his* poetic expectations, Hardy nevertheless recognizes the girl's thoughts as *her* genuine self-expression, as the 'inner themes and inner poetries' of her life.

In 'The Milestone by the Rabbit-Burrow' Hardy again makes a joke of subjectivity, and of the 'pathetic fallacy', by which people interpret nature according to their own moods or feelings. A rabbit observes people's reactions to a milestone, 'I observe men look/ At a stone, and sigh/ As they pass it by/ To some far goal.' He tries to guess the writing on the milestone by the expressions of the passers-by, and in doing so falls victim to a kind of reverse pathetic fallacy: he interprets the stone's significance in terms of rabbithood.

> Something it says
> To their glancing eyes
> That must distress
> The frail and lame,
> And the strong of frame
> Gladden or surprise.
>
> Do signs on its face
> Declare how far
> Feet have to trace
> Before they gain
> Some blest champaign
> Where no gins are?

Sometimes nature harshly destroys the illusions of those who idealize it. The poet of 'In a Wood' comes, 'city-opprest', to the wood, 'Dreaming that sylvan peace/ Offered the harrowed ease', a 'soft release', a contrast to 'men's unrest'. But he finds in nature the same combat and competition that blights the world of men.

> But, having entered in,
>   Great growths and small
> Show them to men akin –
>   Combatants all!
> Sycamore shoulders oak,
>   Bines the slim sapling yoke,
> Ivy-spun halters choke
>   Elms stout and tall.

The awareness of 'In a Wood' clearly showed the limitations of the pastoral idyll of *Under the Greenwood Tree*. Those limitations enable us to enjoy the comedy in a world where there is virtually 'no enemy but winter and rough weather'. But the limitations of that world were too severe for the novelist of the changing, anxious nineteenth century. Hardy returned to that world in 1874 when he published *Far from the Madding Crowd*, but the novel which

The rural landscape of Dorset had a powerful effect on Hardy.

many consider Hardy's best is a more complicated excursion into the world of rural comedy, reminding us always of the fickleness of nature and human nature, as

well as of the sophistications of society which govern human relationships in the rural community as much as anywhere else.

Victorian farm workers in Dorset. Hardy charted the changes brought about in agricultural methods by the onset of industrialization.

47

2 *Far from the Madding Crowd*

Far from the Madding Crowd, like all of Hardy's succeeding novels, was first published as a serial, in monthly instalments. It appeared from January to December 1874, in the *Cornhill* magazine, and was published in volume form in November of that year. *Far from the Madding Crowd* again employs elements of the pastoral mode, but self-consciously, along with other literary and popular

forms – ballad, melodrama, romance. The structure of the novel follows the pattern of comedy, opening with a would-be lover and his obstinate mistress, developing complications through personal failures of understanding and rivalry in love, and ending, after sensational events carrying tragic content – a mistaken marriage, the death of a wronged woman, jealous murder – happily, with the long-desired marriage. The action takes place over a three-year span, from one December to another, marked out by the seasonal activities of the countryside: lambing, sheep-shearing, haymaking, the swarming of bees, the sheep-fair, and by the seasonal festivals of the human community, notably successive Christmasses. Over this period Gabriel Oak falls through chance misfortune from relative prosperity to poverty and rises again to even greater prosperity and to happiness, through the steadiness of his own conscientious effort and loyalty. Bathsheba Everdene is early on made secure in wealth and status as inheritor of a large farm, but through the emotional experience of error and deepening perception,

The action of the novel follows the seasons of the agricultural year, from lambing to sheep-shearing.

Opposite
'Weatherbury Farm', (Waterston Manor near Puddletown). 'The bower of Oak's new-found mistress, Bathsheba Everdene...told at a glance that, as is so frequently the case, it had once been the manorial hall upon a small estate around it.'

'Little Weatherbury Farm', Boldwood's home (Druce Farm, near Puddletown).

she moves from thoughtless happiness to misery and self-awareness which enable her to realize, in her ultimate marriage to Oak, the richer happiness of a 'substantial affection which arises' out of 'good fellowship – *camaraderie*' in mutual knowledge and self-knowledge, 'the romance growing up in the interstices of a mass of hard prosaic reality'.

Hard prosaic reality mingles with literary effects throughout the novel. When Gabriel's sheep are run off a cliff to their deaths by an over-enthusiastic sheepdog, Hardy labels the grotesque and ramifying disaster 'A Pastoral Tragedy'. The idea of classical pastoral is kept alive in this rural story by references to the literary inspiration; but these call attention by contrast to the reality of the world portrayed. 'Without throwing a

Nymphean tissue over a milkmaid . . . ' Hardy says, emphasizing that Bathsheba's beauty needs no exaggeration. Comically presenting the entertainments at the shearing-supper, Hardy invokes figures from Virgilian pastoral: 'Jacob Smallbury . . . volunteered a ballad as inclusive and interminable as that with which the worthy toper old Silenus amused on a similar occasion the swains Chromis and Mnasylus, and other jolly dogs of his day' (ch. 23).

Ballads and ballad-singing are a familiar part of the rural life presented. Singing enlivens social gatherings, and the stuff of popular ballads and lyrics constitutes for the country folk a kind of history and a reading of real life's familiar situations. The songs at the shearing-supper have significance in relation to the action. Before Smallbury embarks on his interminable ballad, two others have been sung. A song of lost love and one of love in the springtime are unconsciously apt at an occasion where the rejected

'For the shearing-supper a long table was placed on the grass-plot beside the house, the end of the table being thrust over the sill of the wide parlour window and a foot or two into the room. Miss Everdene sat inside the window, facing down the table. She was thus at the head without mingling with the men.' (Far from the Madding Crowd, ch.23)

Oak and the hopeful suitor Boldwood sit together with Bathsheba. That her own contribution is unknowingly prophetic is noted in the book:

> Subsequent events caused one of the verses to be remembered for many months, and even years, by more than one of those who were gathered there:-
>
> For his bride a soldier sought her,
>   And a winning tongue had he:
> On the banks of Allan Water
>   None was gay as she!

Sergeant Troy, when he appears, is as a figure out of a ballad, or the melodrama. The dashing military man who ruins a country maid and who is as susceptible as he is attractive is a type recognizable to Hardy's readers as to the Weatherbury community, 'a gay man . . . a clever young dand', 'quick and trim', with a history of noble blood to enhance the gloss. If Oak's solidity and his natural reliability are signalled by his name and the wrinkles of his smile 'like rays in a rudimentary sketch of the rising

'Never since the broadsword became the national weapon had there been more dexterity shown in its management than by the hands of Sergeant Troy...'(ch.28)

52

sun', Troy, 'brilliant in brass and scarlet' is immediately seen as a man of carelessness, instability and seductiveness. That Troy should end up playing the highwayman Dick Turpin in 'The Royal Hippodrome Performance of Turpin's Ride to York and the Death of Black Bess' is fitting, and points neatly to his known vices of pretence, dishonesty and display. Melodramatic elements attend Troy's role in the novel's plot. The seduction of Bathsheba through the display of the sword exercise, the betrayal of Fanny Robin after the mistake of the wrong church episode, and the sensational shooting of Troy by the frenzied Boldwood are all dramatic incidents. They generate understanding and advance the plot while allowing the soldier's presentation in the novel to remain typical and superficial.

If Oak and Troy are characterized through use of the conventional or typical, Boldwood, a more complicated figure, in his passionate obsessiveness and puritanical reserve, is nevertheless also sketched in for us through allusion and reference to the classical epic and dramatic genres. Hardy, casually and calculatedly, makes us aware of the potential in this book's events for tragedy and comedy. For instance, having caused Bathsheba to blush

Gabriel Oak (the actor Alan Bates): 'His Christian name was Gabriel, and on working days he was a young man of sound judgment, easy motions, proper dress, and general good character.' (ch.1)

and flee, 'with an air between that of Tragedy and Comedy
Gabriel returned to his work'. Gabriel's neutral air is quite
different from Boldwood's tensely guarded 'equilibrium'.
'If an emotion possessed him at all, it ruled him; . . . he was
serious throughout all.' His absoluteness, no less than his
inability to see 'absurd sides to the follies of life' – in other
words, his lack of comic awareness – associate him with
tragedy. Hardy underlines the point. 'Being a man who
read all the dramas of life seriously, if he failed to please
when they were comedies, there was no frivolous
treatment to reproach him for when they chanced to end
tragically.' Boldwood's life-drama, nestling beside the
melodramatic events of Troy's career, within the comedy
of Oak's triumph, is unredeemably tragic. The classical
epic provides an image for this sad but dangerous,
doomed figure who has no home in the natural world of
healthy sexuality or the literary world of pastoral
romance: his disappointed 'dark form' walks the hills 'like
an unhappy Shade in the Mournful Fields by Acheron'.

Bathsheba is likened in the book to a pastoral beauty and a ballad heroine, but her presentation is not that of a typical heroine, just as her social role as 'Farmer Everdene' is not typical of women of her age and place. In observing Bathsheba's character, Hardy examines not only the errors of her youth and impulsiveness, but the disadvantages of

In portraying Bathsheba as 'Farmer Everdene', Hardy explores the position of women in a predominantly male world.

a woman's position, and especially those discovered by one who tries to make her way in a masculine society on its own terms. Bathsheba is a more complicated figure than Fancy Day. Hardy calls hers 'an impulsive nature under a deliberative aspect'. She is not a flirt, though an act of flirtatious folly initiates the tragic events of her experience. She is not deceitful; indeed, if the 'Vanity' of which Oak accuses her encourages her mistakes, her honesty brings her near to greater danger in trying to rectify them. Not loving Boldwood, yet, 'she had a strong feeling that, having been the one to begin the game, she ought in honesty to accept the consequences'. The impulsive, or intuitive aspect of Bathsheba prevents her seeking marriage for its own sake, or marrying without love. But this aspect makes her susceptible to the advances and attractions of Troy, who arouses her sexuality, subverting her customary understanding and her otherwise forceful will.

> Bathsheba loved Troy in the way that only self-reliant women love when they abandon their self-reliance ... Her love was entire as a child's, and though warm as summer it was fresh as spring. Her culpability lay in her making no attempt to control feeling by subtle and careful inquiry into consequences.

> (ch. 29)

The imagery of childhood and nature signifies the healthiness of Bathsheba's impulse; what is faulty is its object, and in this case she is unable to appeal 'to her understanding for deliverance from her whims'. Marriage to the faithless Troy proves not merely a disappointment to her hopes, but a violation of her own faith and of that natural impulse. Hardy forcefully presents the revulsion which precedes her final repulse by Troy: 'Her pride was indeed brought low by despairing discoveries of her spoilation by marriage with a less pure nature than her own'. A similar 'revulsion in her sentiments' will overtake Grace Melbury in *The Woodlanders* when she understands 'that she had made a frightful mistake in her marriage', bringing 'degradation to herself' (ch. 29).

Far from the Madding Crowd scrutinizes the terms under which men and women meet, socially and in marriage. Aspects of the marital relation are noted by the narrator.

Possession is the legal and moral basis for marriage: 'Ordinary men take wives because possession is not possible without marriage, and . . . ordinary women accept husbands because marriage is not possible without possession'(ch. 20). Bathsheba, who 'Until she had met Troy . . . had been proud of her position as a woman', finds herself 'conquered'. Bathsheba has trespassed on the male privilege and desired to possess Troy, 'In the turmoil of her anxiety for her lover she had agreed to marry him'; her reward is the bitterness of knowing herself an unvalued

'As for Bathsheba, she had changed. She was sitting on the floor beside the body of Troy, his head pillowed in her lap, where she had herself lifted it.' (ch.54)

possession, and possessor of nothing, as Troy says, 'I am not morally yours'. The antithesis of such contracts of possession, such binding but unnatural relationships, is the 'substantial affection' Hardy praises at the novel's end: 'good fellowship . . . occurring through similarity of pursuits', the compound of passion and friendship which 'proves itself the only love which is strong as death – that love which many waters cannot quench, nor the floods drown . . .'

In addition to these narratorial comments, however, the novel dramatically explores Bathsheba's dilemma and, through it, the position of women. The novel is a mirror of the world where the law and language are men's. With the possible comic exception of Laban Tall's wife, women in the novel are quiet or ineffective in their speech. Fanny Robin keeps her needs a secret, and her pleadings are futile. Liddy Smallbury contradicts herself, trying to say not what she thinks or knows, but what her mistress wants to hear. Bathsheba's communications with Boldwood are wilfully misinterpreted; he refuses to accept the insincerity of the joke Valentine and the sincerity of her rejection alike.

'...the fire was made up in the large long hall into which the staircase descended, and all encumbrances were cleared out for dancing.' (ch. 52)

His desire assumes without justification an emotional possession of Bathsheba as absolute as the legal one marriage would confer upon him. Boldwood plays upon a sense of moral law deep in a girl whose bankrupt father had compensated for unorthodox natural impulses by embracing an exaggerated and aggressive piety. Bathsheba lacks the language as well as the emotional strength to resist Boldwood's 'coercion'. 'It is difficult for a woman to define her feelings in language which is chiefly made by men to express theirs', she protests. Muted by the unavailability of an effective language itself, Bathsheba is prey to the manipulations of her suitors and even to the self-perplexity of one in situations for which ready definitions and available remedies are lacking. At the end of the book, the verbal comedy of Bathsheba's awkward interview with Gabriel in his house, which ends in her indirect proposal, allows understanding to emerge despite linguistic confusion or hesitation, but continues to emphasize the oppressive effect of social convention, which dictates what the woman cannot and the man must say in such a position.

> '"Too - s-s-soon" were the words I used.'
> 'I must beg your pardon for correcting you, but you said "too absurd", and so do I.'
> 'I beg your pardon too!' she returned, with tears in her eyes. '"Too soon" was what I said . . . I only meant, "too soon" . . .'.
> Gabriel looked her long in the face . . . 'Bathsheba,' he said tenderly and in surprise, and coming closer; 'If I only knew one thing – whether you would allow me to love you and win you, and marry you after all – If I only knew that!'
> 'But you never will know', she murmured.
> 'Why?'
> 'Because you never ask.'
>
> (ch. 56)

The narrative of the novel respects Bathsheba's integrity and her privacy. If she lacks a language to describe her feelings in a man's world, the male author knows that an omniscient record of the woman's thoughts is unavailable to him. Like the characters surrounding her in the novel, therefore, he watches Bathsheba and conveys her to us

dramatically, recording her spoken words, her gestures, and comments made about her. In doing this he tells us something of the un-verbal quality of the girl's responses: 'Had her utmost thoughts in this direction been distinctly worded (and by herself they never were) . . . ', but again also something of women's position. It is Bathsheba's fate as a woman, especially as a beautiful woman, to be an observed object. Indeed her awareness of herself is largely shaped by self-observation as well as sensitivity to the ways she is seen by others. Hardy notes this dramatically in the opening scene. Gabriel secretly watches Bathsheba secretly smiling at herself in a mirror. Later he watches her through a chink in the roof of the cattle-shed, and again spies on her equestrian gymnastics through a loophole in his own hut. The narrative uses her behaviour when unconscious of being watched to reveal Bathsheba to Oak and to us. In doing so it establishes a distance between us and the girl at the same time that it enables us to invade her privacy. We join Gabriel and the narrator in watching Bathsheba; for us, as for these male presences, she will always be other, readable only by externals. Even in the moments of our most intense awareness of Bathsheba's state of mind or emotions Hardy preserves this distance, recording what is to be deduced from physical manifestations. Thus when Troy kisses her after the sword-exercise, we are told,

'Gabriel had glanced up in intense surprise, quelled its expression, and looked down again. Bathsheba turned the winch, and Gabriel applied the shears.' (ch.20)

> That minute's interval had brought the blood beating into her face, set her stinging as if aflame to the very hollows of her feet, and enlarged emotion to a compass which quite swamped thought. It had brought . . . a stream of tears. She felt like one who has sinned a great sin.
>
> (ch. 28)

And when he has left her,

> Directly he had gone, Bathsheba burst into great sobs – dry-eyed sobs . . . But she determined to repress all evidences of feeling . . . She chafed to and fro in rebelliousness, like a caged leopard; her whole soul was in arms, and the blood fired her face.
>
> (ch. 41)

61

The seemingly harmless act of watching becomes an important kind of interaction in the book, however. Bathsheba as a woman is sensitive to being a passive object of observation; 'I've been through it, Liddy, . . . it was as bad as being married – eyes everywhere'. Observation is physically experienced and it, too, may become an act of possession. Even Gabriel's admiration suggests violation: 'Rays of male vision seem to have a tickling effect upon virgin faces in rural districts; she brushed hers with her hand, as if Gabriel had been irritating its pink surface by actual touch . . . '. It is because Boldwood fails to return 'evidences of her power to attract', as a flattering mirror might, that Bathsheba notices him, 'Women seem to have eyes in their ribbons for such matters', and disastrously calls attention to herself with the thoughtless Valentine. Her 'triumph' is at first to win his observation, 'His eyes, she knew, were following her everywhere'. No sooner does he see her, though, than Boldwood substitutes for the real woman his own idealized vision of her, '. . . there was hardly awakened a thought in Boldwood that sorry household realities appertained to her, or that she, like all others, had moments of commonplace . . . '. She becomes the object of his fantasies, possessed according to the law of his desire, more estranged from his understanding than when she was merely unnoticed. Troy in his turn is captivated by her beauty and then blames her for not being what his fancy had made her. Only Oak, who observes her thoughtfully and modifies his judgment by sifting the varied evidence of her character, ultimately meets Bathsheba in the realm of her own real self and of her wordless expression: 'They spoke very little of their mutual feelings; pretty phrases and warm expressions being probably unnecessary between such tried friends' (ch. 56).

Bathsheba stands out in a novel where other characters – even major ones – are typical. She shares the female burdens of passivity and inarticulacy with Fanny Robin, but whereas the sterotypical Fanny becomes the apotheosis of these qualities in death, Bathsheba remains alive and unpredictable, challenging the reader through her unorthodox actions and the very unconventional depth of her wordless responses, 'The parson's words spread into the heavy air with a sad unperturbed cadence, and Gabriel shed an honest tear. Bathsheba seemed

'Bathsheba did not at once perceive that the grand tomb and disturbed grave were Fanny's . . . Then . . . she read the words with which the inscription opened . . .'
(ch. 46)

unmoved', to discover the real beyond the typical. Tess's
ringing challenge to Alec d'Urberville, 'Did it never strike
your mind that what every woman says some women may
feel?' (*Tess*, ch. 12) is a more tragic echo of Bathsheba's

wrestle with the constraints of men's language and men's generalizations, of her struggle to resist pre-judgement by marketplace observers, malthouse gossips, suitors and readers alike. Bathsheba says 'I *hate* to be thought men's property'. Her struggle is against the social conventions that generated laws that made women and their property their husbands', and shaped the obstructive divorce laws against which Hardy would protest in *The Woodlanders* and *Jude the Obscure*. Bathsheba's character as a 'self-reliant', 'deliberative', and sexually aware woman is a challenge to 'the doll of English fiction' which Hardy vowed to 'demolish'.

The recognitions which threaten the comedy in *Far from the Madding Crowd* – of the darkness or irrationality of the human psyche, of social snobbery and of social and legal inequality, of nature's own capacity for destruction – grow more potent in Hardy's succeeding works. As Hardy looked hard and unsentimentally at nature, the awarenesses seen in poems such as 'In a Wood' grew, and pastoral comedy proved to be no longer an appropriate form.

Nature harboured the Darwinian struggle, where species and members of species competed for survival, and rural people's lives were hard and often as stunted as the forest trees. Such a vision is found in *The Woodlanders* (published in 1887).

> On older trees still than these huge lobes of fungi grew like lungs. Here, as everywhere, the Unfulfilled Intention, which makes life what it is, was as obvious as it could be among the depraved crowds of a city slum. The leaf was deformed, the curve was crippled, the taper was interrupted; the lichen ate the vigour of the stalk, and the ivy slowly strangled to death the promising sapling.

As Hardy contemplated such visions of nature and human nature happy resolutions such as that of *Far from the Madding Crowd* diminished among the endings of his novels. As the conventions of pastoral proved inadequate to a realistic picture of the world, Hardy's treatment of nature became more subtle, often more symbolic, and the technique of his novels moved away from the conventional forms of comedy and tragedy to adopt more shocking and experimental shapes.

3 *The Mayor of Casterbridge*

As Hardy moved from the pastoral he moved from the comic, too. *The Return of the Native* (1878) has a tragic plot growing out of misplaced or misunderstood aspirations; social ambitions clash with humane ones; proud, determined people, each with his or her own peculiar sense of superiority, are fated to discover the limitations of mortality and the pain of thwarted desire. Hardy's next major 'tragic' novel was *The Mayor of Casterbridge*. Its focus is on one man, whose eminence is signalled by the book's title and whose downfall is marked by the passing of the title to his one-time employee and chief rival. In the character of Michael Henchard Hardy created a 'tragic hero, along lines reminiscent of the classical pattern described by Aristotle – an eminent man falls from happiness to misery as a result of an error (*hamartia*). The grotesque, but historically-based, early error of Henchard in selling his wife precipitates a series of events witnessing the rise to civic eminence, wealth and self-esteem and the subsequent decline of the one-time mayor. The fall, like the rise, is the effect not of a unique and malign fate, but of the character of the man – stubborn and generous, impulsive, slow to adapt and yet strikingly resilient – in combination with circumstances outside himself which provoke or precipitate action.

The novel is set in familiar Hardy country. Like classical tragedy it takes place in one location, the town of Casterbridge and its environs. The place, however, has a

The Mayor of Casterbridge

by Thomas Hardy.
Author of "Far from the Madding Crowd", "A Pair of Blue Eyes", &c.

Chapter I.

One evening of late summer, before the present century had reached its middle-age, a young man & woman, the latter carrying a child, were approaching the large village of Weydon-Priors on foot. They were plainly but not ill clad, though the thick hoar of dust which had accumulated on their shoes & clothing from an obviously long journey lent a disadvantageous shabbiness

Hardy's manuscript of The Mayor of Casterbridge. *He began writing the novel early in 1884.*

vastness about it which is not merely geographical, but historical. The action of the book radiates out from the market square of Casterbridge of the 1840s to the surrounding landmarks of river and medieval priory, Roman burial-ground and the impressive Ring, one of the 'finest Roman amphitheatres', 'accessible from every part of the town', with an awesome vastness and a history of 'sinister' and 'sanguinary' uses, to the 'prehistoric fort called Mai Dun, of huge dimensions and many ramparts, within or upon whose enclosures a human being . . . was but an insignificant speck'. The landscape itself tells a tale of rise and fall, of civilizations giving way to new civilizations, manifesting the tokens of past Empire in a time of new Empire. As the physical landscape belittles the human in it, so the temporal setting of the novel dwarfs the moment of the individual human life. And yet it is on that moment that we focus. The time-span of the book is just over twenty years, from the time Henchard sells his wife to the time of his death, but the focus is on the latter two of those years. In that time Casterbridge itself witnesses change. When Elizabeth-Jane arrives in Casterbridge she sees a square borough 'untouched by the

Maumbury Rings, south of Dorchester. Originally a Neolithic henge, the rings were made into an amphitheatre by the Romans.

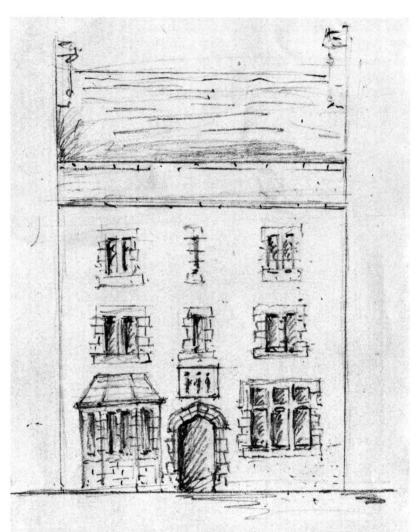

The Three Mariners Inn.
Dorchester.

Drawn by Thomas Hardy
as he remembered it.

faintest sprinkle of modernism'. It is an anomaly, an 'indistinct mass of human commerce and habitation, set in the midst of miles of rotund down and concave field', a place at whose boundaries 'country and town met at a mathematical line'. But this Casterbridge has changed in its relation to the surrounding countryside during the time spanned by the book's opening chapters. Returning to the agricultural fair at Weydon-Priors after twenty years, Susan Newson finds that event much diminished: 'the real business of the fair had considerably dwindled. The new periodical great markets of neighbouring towns were beginning to interfere seriously with the trade carried on here for centuries'. Casterbridge itself is a beneficiary of this commercial change: 'the agricultural and pastoral character of the people upon whom the town depended for its existence was shown by the class of objects

Opposite *'The Three Mariners – whose two prominent Elizabethan gables, bow window, and passage light could be seen . . . '* (The Mayor of Casterbridge).

Agricultural fair, Stallbridge, Dorset, 1893.

Agricultural workers harvesting. In Far from the Madding Crowd *Gabriel saves Bathsheba's valuable wheat ricks from destruction by fire and by rain.*

displayed in the shop windows'. If the shift of population and agricultural commerce from the surrounding villages to the market-towns signals that an older rural way of life has passed, a perceptible 'sprinkle of modernism' accompanies Donald Farfrae's arrival in Casterbridge. His very travels are a sign of changing times; he has left his highland homeland with the intention of emigrating, as many ambitious young men did in the early nineteenth century, and he finds good employment in the south of the country as a result of his skill in modern methods of wheat-growing. Advancing agricultural methods bring Henchard and Farfrae together, and later mark their severance and associate themselves with their contrasting fates. Gossip comments on the contrast of the traditional and the new:

[Henchard's] accounts were like a bramble-wood when Mr. Farfrae came. He used to reckon his sacks by chalk strokes all in a row like garden-palings, measure his ricks by stretching with his arms, weigh his trusses by a lift, judge his hay by a chaw, and settle the price with a curse. But now this accomplished young man does it all by ciphering and mensuration.

(ch. 16)

The invasion of modernism upon the Casterbridge scene is epitomized by the arrival in the town market of a mechanized seed drill.

> It was the new-fashioned agricultural implement called a horse-drill, till then unknown, in its modern shape, in this part of the country, where the venerable seed-lip was still used for sowing as in the days of the Heptarchy. Its arrival created about as much sensation in the corn-market as a flying machine would create at Charing Cross.
>
> (ch. 24)

To Lucetta it looks like 'a sort of agricultural piano'; Henchard ridicules it; Farfrae says it 'will revolutionize

A Dorset farmer using a Broadcast seed drill to sow seeds.

sowing heerabout'; and Elizabeth-Jane recognizes that in its doing so, 'the romance of the sower is gone for good'. Each character's response is in keeping with his or her nature and interests, but perhaps Elizabeth-Jane's dialogue with Farfrae best catches the book's complicated response to the changes – historical and personal – which it chronicles. The old possesses the charm of romance, the affection which early associations bring, and Hardy was sensitive to this. In part, the novel is an elegy for the passing of a pre-mechanical rural England. But is does not argue for a turning back. The old is also associated with inefficiency, superstition, with the barbarity that permits Henchard to sell his wife in public and the arbitrariness which makes him a tyrant at home and at his place of business. It seems clear that Farfrae's mistakes will never be so disastrous, nor his passions so strong as Henchard's. The modernism which he heralds is neither good nor bad in itself; it is merely inevitable, and like the old methods will remain to be judged by its results.

In Henchard's character our mixed feelings towards change are focused. We are impatient with his stubbornness and impulsiveness and yet we admire his loyalty and sympathize with the regret that inevitably follows on his impulsive, self-destructive acts. His possessiveness, pride and competitiveness are compelling, set beside Farfrae's mild opportunism. We increasingly suspect that he is doomed by his character,

which Hardy calls Faustian, 'a vehement gloomy being who had quitted the ways of vulgar men, without light to guide him on a better way' (in allusion to the overreaching hero of tragedies by Marlowe in the sixteenth century and Goethe in the nineteenth). That he is ill-treated by chance we see, as 'the persistence of the unforeseen' brings (in the returns of Susan, Lucetta, the furmity-woman and Newson, in the misfortunes of the grown wheat, the mistaken weather forecast, and numerous coincidental misunderstandings) situations which try, and defeat him. As we learn, along with Elizabeth-Jane, of his last days, wandering the heath in sorrow, like King Lear, with Abel Wittle for 'poor fond fool', we mingle admiration for his strength and for his familiar mixed character, 'he was kind-like to mother when she were here below, though 'a was rough to me', with pity for his loneliness.

The carefully constructed novel returns us both to its starting point and to a new state of 'tranquility'. Henchard wanders to die out into a countryside as empty of its former life as himself. Elizabeth-Jane and Farfrae have wed (an event looked forward to from earlier chapters). The other characters have, through death or relocation, left the story. The final remarks concern Elizabeth-Jane. Like Gabriel Oak, Elizabeth-Jane has been throughout a character able to adapt to her fate without compromising her integrity. She has provided a contrast to her timid mother, and to the ambitious and defensive Lucetta, a woman subject to whims and emotion. Elizabeth-Jane's steadiness, unselfishness and native intelligence have made her a sensitive reader of the world of chance and change which so baffled her stepfather. All these characters appear static, however, compared to Henchard. Our interest remains firmly focused on the mayor who is a hero only in the sense of having that capacity to arrest our attention and provoke our thought. Henchard's tragedy allows us to explore our own resistance to change and to feel the need for a human sense of importance. It shows us the interaction of the historical moment and the personal. It teaches us that tragedy may occur as a result of a perspective too intently and entirely focused on the self, its would-be power, and its desires. But it also shows us that we are moved to admiration by the effort of an infinitesimal creature, amidst the vastnesses of inhuman space and time, to be great.

Opposite *King's Arms Hotel, Dorchester. 'The building was the chief hotel in Casterbridge – namely the King's Arms. A spacious bow-window projected into the street over the main portico, and from the open sashes came the babble of voices, the jingle of glasses, and the drawing of cords'. (ch. 5)*

4 Hardy's Later Work and Thought

In later books Hardy continued to use the natural world and rural settings to register changes taking place in the social order or the economic structure of the country. Nature is used to provide an analogy for human states of mind and of physical well- or ill- being and Hardy questions nature itself, looking for ways to understand the world in which human dramas play themselves out. Grace Melbury, in *The Woodlanders*, who has suffered from her father's ambitions and her husband's unfaithfulness, and

'trees close together, wrestling for existence' (The Woodlanders).

76

has witnessed the economic and emotional defeats suffered by her honest lover, has a vision of a nature predatory in parts, parasitic in others, and hosting a battle of survival:

> From the other window all she could see were more trees, in jackets of lichen and stockings of moss. At their roots were stemless yellow fungi like lemons and apricots, and tall fungi with more stem than stool. Next were more trees close together, wrestling for existence, their branches disfigured with wounds resulting from their mutual rubbings and blows. It was the struggle between these neighbours that she had heard in the night. Beneath them were the rotting stumps of those of the group that had been vanquished long ago. . .
>
> (ch. 42)

'How it rained/When we worked at Flintcomb Ash/And could not stand upon the hill/Trimming swedes for the slicing-mill . . .'
('We Field-Women')

In *Tess of the d'Urbervilles* contrasting scenes of the lush, fragrant, sun-drenched Talbothays Dairy where Tess is happy and secure, and finds her love reciprocated by Angel Clare, are contrasted with the cold, hard fields of Flintcomb Ash, where, after her abandonment by Angel, Tess and the other itinerant workers are worked to

Hardy's 'Christminster': Oxford High Street.

Opposite *'The pleasures of bicycling were now at their highest appreciation . . . He was not a long-distance cyclist, as was natural at fifty-nine, never exceeding forty to fifty miles a day, but he kept vigorously going within the limit . . .' (The Life of Thomas Hardy)*

exhaustion feeding the steam threshing machine. In *Jude the Obscure* the question is asked: *is* 'Nature's law . . . mutual butchery'? As nature becomes a less settled background in these novels, the one-place book gives way to novels with peripatetic plots. Wanderings give structure to *Tess, A Laodicean, Jude*.

We tend to think of Hardy as a tragic novelist, but through most of his novel-writing career he alternated plots with what we can term comic and tragic structure. That career which began disappointingly with *The Poor Man and the Lady* extended to fourteen novels, six volumes of stories, and nearly 1,000 poems. Nevertheless it is true that as Hardy became increasingly successful and well-known, his novels addressed themselves more urgently and uncomfortably to questions of social injustice, to the presentation of the signs and victims of change in a 'modern' world, and to the great questions of where the responsibility for human unhappiness lay. The culmination of this progress was *Jude the Obscure*, published in 1895. Hardy described the novel as a 'dramatic story' of 'the labours of a poor student to get a University degree, and . . . the tragic issues of two bad marriages' (*Life*, p. 271). The story of Jude's failures becomes an examination of crucial social, moral and sexual issues and is one of Hardy's most powerful works.

'Jude . . . went to a dreary, strange, flat scene . . . where he had never been before.'
(Jude the Obscure)

He called it 'a book all contrasts', emphasizing 'the contrast between the ideal life a man wished to lead, and the squalid real life he was fated to lead' (*Life*, p. 272). Contrasts structure the novel: between characters, between places, and between established thought and 'modern' opinions. Its technique also embraces a struggle between the convention of Victorian realist fiction and the powerful innovations, in imagery, outspoken dialogue, and the book's circular plot which Hardy found necessary to enforce his passionate 'questionings'.

Jude was greeted by an 'onslaught' of 'vituperative' criticism (*Life*, p. 270) which depressed Hardy more than the considerable appreciative comment could cheer him. He wrote no more novels (*The Well-Beloved*, published in 1897, had been largely written earlier), preferring to embrace poetry as a finer medium and a better one for showing the world's shortcomings or life's injustices. His first volume, *Wessex Poems* (1898), contained many poems exploring failure, regret, missed opportunity, or nature's cruelties. This tendency led critics of Hardy's own day to call him a 'pessimist', a label which he denied, but which has remained a prominent note in Hardy criticism.

Hardy always firmly insisted that his work as a whole represented no coherent system of thought, no 'philosophy of life'. 'Positive views on the Whence and the Wherefore of things have never been advanced by this pen as a consistent philosophy . . . ', he said, 'the sentiments . . . have been stated truly to be mere impressions of the moment, and not convictions or arguments' (Preface to the Wessex Edition of 1912). This is not to say that Hardy

Sherborne Abbey, Dorset. Fan-vaulting in the nave is one of the striking features of the Perpendicular style of Gothic architecture which dominates the Abbey.

conceived of his poems or his novels as irrelevant or irresponsible. 'Unadjusted impressions', he said, ' have their value, and the road to a true philosophy of life seems to lie in humbly recording diverse readings of its phenomena as they are forced upon us by chance and change' (Preface: *Poems of the Past and the Present*). This sense of the importance of *different* experiences and differing responses to experience helps to explain the variety in Hardy's fictions.

To understand Hardy's style in poetry and fiction and the ideas behind it, it is helpful to go back to his involvement with Gothic architecture, for Hardy himself drew an analogy between the style of those buildings and the kind of poetry he tried to write. Gothic buildings seemed to Hardy to represent a style inspired by nature

81

and realizing ideals beyond the imagination of their creators. He answered critics who objected to the 'irregular' forms of his poetry that:

> He had fortified himself in his opinion by thinking of the analogy of architecture, between which art and that of poetry he had discovered . . . that there existed a close and curious parallel, both arts . . . having to carry a rational content inside their artistic form. He knew that in architecture cunning irregularity is of enormous worth, and it is obvious that he carried on into his verse . . . the Gothic art-principle . . . of spontaneity . . . resulting in the 'unforeseen' (as it has been called) character of his metres and stanzas, that of stress rather than of syllable, poetic texture rather than poetic veneer . . .
>
> (*Life* , p. 301)

The Gothic 'spontaneity' which Hardy speaks of lies partly in the variety of language and of verse forms in his poetry. Varied metre and rhythm, literal observation mixed with simile and metaphor, repetition, inversion and alliteration, all enliven this description of 'Snow in the Suburbs':

> Every branch big with it,
> Bent every twig with it;
> Every fork like a white web-foot;
> Every street and pavement mute:
> Some flakes have lost their way, and grope back
>   upward, when
> Meeting those meandering down they turn and descend
>   again.
> The palings are glued together like a wall,
> And there is no waft of wind with the fleecy fall.

'Irregularity' can also be seen in such awkwardnesses as the archaisms in 'But that I fain would wot of shuns my sense' ('A Sign Seeker'), or this early attempt to write self-mockingly about his youthful hopes in the classical sapphic metre:

> 'Thwart my wistful way did a damsel saunter,
> Fair, albeit unformed to be all-eclipsing;
> 'Maiden meet,' held I, 'till arise my forefelt
>   Wonder of women.'

Gothic irregularity is also reflected in the grotesque scenes or images, the dreadful coincidences or shocking twists of fate in his novels. Examples are the hideous gargoyle spitting on Fanny Robin's grave in *Far from the Madding Crowd*, the effigy which presents Henchard with an image of his mortality in *The Mayor of Casterbridge*, or the end of *A Pair of Blue Eyes* where two lovers travelling to seek out the woman they both love discover that they have been sharing a train with her coffin. But Gothic spontaneity also resides importantly in the dramatic quality of his poems and novels. Hardy described his poems as 'a series of feelings and fancies written down in widely differing moods and circumstances'. He called the poems 'personative' – that is, they impersonated those different moods called forth by a variety of circumstances.

The sort of scene that could have inspired Hardy to write 'Snow in the Suburbs'.

Winchester Cathedral: a grotesque roof boss depicting an ancient pagan giant.

He had a similar idea of his novels: *Jude the Obscure* he called 'a series of seemings, or personal impressions'. These 'seemings' or impressions – of the voices in his poems and the characters in his novels – are some of those 'unadjusted impressions' which when recorded, accumulated, provide in Hardy's work the basis for a philosophy of life.

Hardy's idea of a philosophy of life itself was something like a Gothic structure. The Gothic, John Ruskin said, raised edifices of beauty and integrity 'out of fragments full of imperfection and betraying that imperfection at every touch'. Hardy knew that imperfection was inevitable in nature. He knew that human knowledge was, and would remain, imperfect, limited. The poet – or the novelist – attempts to embody human experience, 'All the vast various moils that mean a world alive' ('A Sign-Seeker'), in his works. His view of that experience will always be limited, partial, questioning. The record of mortal experience is always incomplete – no artist can presume to complete it without falsifying. The only way towards completeness, then, is through a proliferation of the bits – the impressions, the seemings, and their records. The artist who records experiences, impressions, questionings, builds an edifice 'out of fragments full of

Worcester Cathedral. The west front of this medieval Gothic cathedral is almost entirely Victorian, the building having been restored between 1857 and 1874.

St. Pancras station, an example of Victorian Gothic style. When the railway was put through the churchyard in 1866 Hardy was deputed by Blomfield to see that the job of removing the coffins was properly done. One evening a coffin fell apart, revealing a skeleton and two skulls. Years later Blomfield greeted Hardy with 'Do you remember how we found the man with two heads at St. Pancras?'

imperfection'. Those fragments, those 'diverse readings of life's phenomena' as they appear in the shifting contexts of 'chance and change', when allowed to combine, amass, and grow *become* the Gothic structure, the truest record of life, holding our uncertainties and imperfections as well as our will to understand. Like the Gothic structure these 'readings' have their root in nature – both external nature which may be their occasion or subject, and the impulse of the human perceiver – and like the Gothic, they aspire beyond nature. For the constant aim of Hardy's 'questionings', his recorded 'readings' of *real* life is an ultimate and impossible *ideal* understanding. Hardy seeks to understand the world which is a place of contradiction, injustice, pain and incongruity. And he tries to know how things can be improved. 'Such "questionings" in the exploration of reality,' Hardy says, may appear as pessimism when dramatized in a poem like 'Hap' or 'Yell'ham-Wood's Story, or in a novel like *The Mayor* or *Tess* or *Jude* – but, he says, such questionings are 'the first step towards the soul's betterment and the body's also' (*Apology: Late Lyrics and Earlier*).

If we scrutinize Hardy's works we find the pessimism itself qualified, the route to betterment hinted at. The idea that fate may not be malign, but *neutral*, throws the ball into our court. In 'Hap' the poet discovers that he is not tormented by a cruel power: his sorrows are all *chance* (Old English: 'hap'), and beyond understanding. The idea of our failure or incapacity to understand the workings of a universe which does things *so much worse* than we would do them is present in the novels as well as the poetry. Hardy throws out provocative questions. *Is* happiness 'the occasional episode in a general drama of pain'? If the terms were applied to Michael Henchard we might think so. But they are part of what Elizabeth-Jane's experience '*seems*' to have taught her. And despite past pain, Elizabeth-Jane is 'forced to class herself among the fortunate' at the end of *The Mayor of Casterbridge*. Tess thinks that ours is a blighted

Stonehenge. 'Older than the centuries; older than the d'Urbervilles!' (Tess)

planet – and so it would seem from her experience – yet is it a 'President of the Immortals', as Hardy ironically suggests, who has cast the blight and who 'sports' with Tess, or is the fault in human nature whose imperfections are blazoned in that book?

It appears that there are several ways of looking at these things. From a distance, does it matter if Henchard is foolish, stubborn and gets his come-uppance? Perhaps not much. In the vast amphitheatre or the open countryside who notices him? Up close, it does matter. We see Henchard make others suffer. We see him suffer. His tragedy is great in his eyes and the way he fends off and invites his loss greatly interests us. We may understand his limitations, but his tragedy moves us. It does so because, as fellow humans, we have some humility and human compassion and pride in our kind. Hardy said of *Two on a Tower*, published in 1882, which is about an astronomer and the lady he loves, 'This slightly-built romance was the outcome of a wish to set the emotional history of two infinitesimal lives against the stupendous background of

Maiden Castle, a prehistoric hill fort near Winterbourne St. Martin, Dorset.

the stellar universe, and to impart to readers the sentiment that of these contrasting magnitudes the smaller might be the greater to them as men'. In other words, from a human point of view the fates of ordinary people are important; from the point of view of men and women, the losses of men and women (of opportunity, of aspiration, of hope, of loved ones) are capable of tragic stature. Our humane response to the needs of our fellows was, in Hardy's view, the chief moral good in the universe. This response was what his fictions sought to call forth.

'the President of the Immortals . . . had ended his sport with Tess.'

Hardy did not believe in an all-knowing God who stood behind the imperfect created world which Hardy saw around him. He had the notion that there is in nature an impulse which motivates the world's existence. All of nature participates in this impulse. The human consciousness – that of the race and of every individual human – is part of that general consciousness; human intention and desire are part of that intrinsic intent which motivates the world's development. The only way that Hardy could explain the failure of this force to organize things better was by assuming that it *had not yet* a fully evolved consciousness. But if consciousness were still evolving, there might still be a chance. Maybe, some eons hence, nature – with humanity pre-eminent in it – would achieve a perfected consciousness. In aid of this, therefore, the consciousness of humans must act rightly now, must move nature to the ends we would desire, the ends we would call humane.

Hardy makes a half-joking allusion to this possibility in the poem 'God's Education'. 'God' here represents the forces which seem so wrong, so unjust to humans – of mortality, and loss. This 'God', or his agent Time, causes a young woman to die. Humankind protests:

> Said I: 'We call that cruelty –
>   We, your poor mortal kind.'
> He mused. 'The thought is new to me.
> Forsooth, though I men's master be,
> Theirs is the teaching mind!'

'Theirs is the teaching mind.' What humankind has to teach is what Hardy called 'lovingkindness'. Lovingkindness meant what it said: love of others, of other people, beasts, nature. There are examples of Hardy's humaneness in his works: in the act of writing Henchard's tragedy, of echoing and focusing the plight of so many who suffered under the nineteenth-century marriage laws in *The Woodlanders* and *Jude the Obscure*, in his poems urging kindness to animals and – more strikingly – in much of his war poetry. Poems written at the time of the Boer War found 'glory and war-mightiness' valueless compared to 'deeds of home' ('The Souls of the Slain'; see also 'The Sick Battle God', 'Departure', 'A Christmas Ghost Story'), and Hardy was unusual among noncombatants of his generation in noting early the barbarism and futility of the First World War, even though he felt that England must be defended. (See, for instance, 'The Pity of It', 'Often When Warring', 'Them and Us', and others.)

At the end of Hardy's epic drama The *Dynasts*, the last word on the fate of humanity is given to the choruses of supernatural spirits. They question the un-caringness of the 'all-mover'. The Pities ask 'shall not Its blindness break?/ Yea, must not Its heart awake,/ Promptly tending/ To Its mending/ In a genial germing purpose,

Soldiers on the Western Front. Hardy noted the futility of the First World War.

and for loving-kindness' sake?' If the consciousness of the universe will not wake to humaneness, the life of the universe might better not be. *The Dynasts* ends – unusually and outspokenly for Hardy – with a 'stirring' that 'thrills the air/ Like to sounds of joyance there/ That the rages/ Of the ages/ Shall be cancelled, and deliverance offered from the darts that were,/ Consciousness the Will informing, till It fashion all things fair!'

Hardy's view of a possible positive evolution, however slow, was never again so forcefully expressed. Indeed the bitterness, the sense of utter failure in *Jude the Obscure* that grows out of and overtakes the novel's message of social need, seems a more real Hardy note. And yet *Jude*, like so many of Hardy's novels, is a striking diagnosis of what is wrong in society and a pointer to better things, Though he claimed to adhere to his 'evolutionary meliorism' as late as 1922, Hardy gave little sign of hope in his latter years.

He was happy in his second marriage to the former Florence Dugdale, nearly forty years younger than Hardy, whom he had married just over a year after Emma's death. Florence was an able writer who had been Hardy's assistant and had proved a needed friend to Emma in her last years. She was herself of a melancholy temperament, but patient and devoted. She understood and protected Hardy's need to cherish his regrets for Emma and to exert his remarkable but diminishing energies to participate in the literary and social circles where his importance was unquestioned, his presence invited, and his opinions solicited.

In his last volume of poetry Hardy seemed to retreat from the need to question, to urge, to record that had driven him throughout a long life. 'We are Getting to the End' is a poem he placed at the end of his last volume. 'We are getting to the end of dreams!' he said.

> We are getting to the end of visioning
> The impossible within this universe,
> Such as that better whiles may follow worse,
> And that our race may mend by reasoning.

Florence Dugdale,
Thomas Hardy's
second wife.

Was it his genuine thought? Was it simply a mood, likely, as ever, to give way to another mood?

In his novels Hardy had offered scope for the reader to learn about human nature in its psychological and social aspects. His characters in their trying or comic situations could prompt us to a fuller understanding of human motive and to an assessment of society's strengths or ills. His novels were capable of moving readers by their dramatic force. His poetry could put the problems of living in a variety of lights, teaching us how influential and inescapable our own subjectivity is. *28*

Thomas Hardy died on 9 January 1911, after an illness culminating in a heart attack. Florence Hardy's conclusion to the *Life*, prepared with the help of notes left by Hardy, records that after his death his face bore a look of 'radiant triumph' and that, 'Later the first radiance passed away, but dignity and peace remained as long as eyes could see the mortal features of Thomas Hardy'. The account finishes, fittingly, with a movement away from the man to the natural scene in a description reminiscent of many in Hardy's novels: 'The dawn of the following day rose in almost unparalleled splendour. Flaming and magnificent the sky stretched its banners over the dark pines that stood sentinel around.' Hardy's poetry is full of self-images. Indeed, he commented on the variety of images one man's

Max Gate, the house on the outskirts of Dorchester which Hardy designed himself and had built by his father and brother. The house had views south to the downs and north to the heath and woodlands around Higher Bockhampton.

lifetime could present to different viewers, or to a viewer at different moments, in the poem 'So Various', which concludes:

Now . . . All these specimens of man,
So various in their pith and plan,
    Curious to say
    Were *one* man. Yea,
    I was all they.

But he knew how he wanted to be remembered. Another autobiographical view of Hardy, another of the images that he prepared for his public, is the poem 'Afterwards'. Again it is quintessentially Hardy, this time a *prospective* retrospect. He looks forward to how people will remember him when he is gone. It is full of the minute observation that was his habit, and the accurate description that was his great skill; the description is of the nature Hardy loved and learned from. The poem embodies his impulse and morality of sympathy:

When the Present has latched its postern behind my
    tremulous stay,
  And the May month flaps its glad green leaves like
    wings,
Delicate- filmed as new-spun silk, will the neighbours
    say,
  'He was a man who used to notice such things'?

If it be in the dusk when, like an eyelid's soundless
    blink,
  The dewfall-hawk comes crossing the shades to alight
Upon the wind- warped upland thorn, a gazer may
    think,
  'To him this must have been a familiar sight.'

If I pass during some nocturnal blackness, mothy and
    warm,
  When the hedgehog travels furtively over the lawn,
One may say, 'He strove that such innocent creatures
    should come to no harm,
  But he could do little for them; and now he is gone.'

If, when hearing that I have been stilled at last, they
    stand at the door,

Watching the full-starred heavens that winter sees,
Will this thought rise on those who will meet my face
     no more,
'He was one who had an eye for such mysteries'?

And will any say when my bell of quittance is heard in
     the gloom,
And a crossing breeze cuts a pause in its outrollings,
Till they rise again, as they were a new bell's boom,
'He hears it not now, but used to notice such things'?

Hardy's reputation, controversial but substantial in his lifetime, was recognized at his death by the immediate seizing of his body for interment in Westminster Abbey. Only his heart was allowed to lie where Hardy had wished his body to, with his family in Stinsford churchyard. His influence on succeeding generations of writers has been great; the novelists George Gissing, D.H. Lawrence and John Cowper Powys, and the poets W.H. Auden, Donald Davie, Philip Larkin and Seamus Heaney are among the well-known writers who have paid tribute to his importance for their writing and in shaping the course of English literature in this century.

Hardy in old age.

Glossary

Acheron   In Greek myth the name of river in Hades, the Underworld.

Alliteration   Repetition of the same sound at the beginning of succcessive or closely connected words.

Analogy   Agreement, similarity; a parallel likeness.

Anomaly   Irregularity of behaviour.

Apothesis   Deification; deified ideal or highest development.

Autobiography   The written story of one's own life *cf.* biography – the written life of another person.

Ballad   A poem in short stanzas narrating a popular story, originally designed to be sung.

Champaign   Stretch of open country, a plain.

Charing Cross   A locality in the City of Westminster, Greater London, where the street called the Strand leads eastward to the City of London from the north end of Whitehall. Charing Cross was often considered the heart of London, from which road distances to other places were measured. It takes its name from the last of the series of 12 crosses erected by Edward I marking the stages of the funeral procession of Queen Eleanor (d. 1290) to Westminster Abbey. The original cross was destroyed during the Civil War and a modern cross, erected in 1863, stands in the forecourt of the Charing Cross railway station.

Chivalric   Having to do with *Chivalry*: medieval knightly system with its own religious, moral and social code. The ideal knightly characteristics were courage, courtesy and readiness to defend the weak.

Classical   Of ancient Latin or Greek standard authors, or art.

Comedy   A literary work, especially a play, less serious than a tragedy, usually having a happy ending. *Romantic comedy*: a play in which love is the central motive of an action which leads to a happy ending (and usually to marriage).

Corn-law agitations   The Corn Laws were English laws restricting importation of grain. They were repealed, after protests, in 1846.

Darwinian Of the ideas of Charles Darwin (1809 –
1882), British naturalist whose theory of evolution
based on natural selection is known as Darwinism.
His theory, derived from documented observations of
evolution, is found in *The Origin of Species by Means of
Natural Selection* (1859) and *The Descent of Man and
Selection in Relation to Sex* (1871). Darwin's theories
have been, somewhat misleadingly, characterized by
the popular phrase 'survival of the fittest'.

Diagnosis Identification of disease by means of
symptoms, or ascertainment of the cause of a fault.

Domicile Dwelling place, home. *Domicilium*: Latin for
home.

Elegy Song of lamentation, especially for the dead;
sometimes used to refer to a lament for what is past.

Eliot, George (1819 – 1880) English novelist. Mary Ann
Evans, whose most famous novels include
Middlemarch (1871-2), *Adam Bede* (1859) and *The Mill
on the Floss* (1860).

Epic Poem narrating continuously the achievements of
a hero or heroes. Classical examples are Homer's
Odyssey and *Iliad*, Virgil's *Aeneid*.

Evolution The process of development.

Evolve To develop by a natural process.

Fain Archaic word meaning willing under the
circumstances to, or left with no alternative but to;
would fain: would be glad to.

Faustian Like Faust, a legendary scholar who gained
superhuman powers by entering into a pact with the
devil. Associated with the idea of a human (usually a
person of learning) who overreaches human powers.

Flying buttress A support built against a wall, slanting
up to the wall from a column, etc.

Generic Characteristic of a genus, class or genre.

Genre Kind or style of literature, e.g. novel, tragedy,
comedy, epic, lyric.

Gin A trap, snare or net.

Hamlet A small village.

Heptarchy Government by seven rulers; supposed
seven kingdoms of Angles and Saxons in Britain in
7th - 8th centuries.

Hippodrome Theatre for various stage entertainments;
or, a circus. The term comes from the Greek and
Roman name for the course for chariot races.

Indigenous Produced naturally in a region; belonging naturally (to).

Intrinsic Belonging naturally, inherent and essential.

Ironic Using irony. *Irony*: the expression of one's meaning by using words which say the opposite, e.g. using words of praise to ridicule; use of language which has an inner meaning for a privileged audience and an outer meaning for the persons addressed; the ill-timed or perverse arrival of an event or circumstance at a moment when it is unsuitable.

Laodicean Person who is lukewarm, especially in religion or politics. From Laodicea in Asia Minor. *Revelation* 3:14 – 16 says 'And to the angel of the church in Laodicea write ... "I know your works: you are neither cold nor hot ... So, because you are lukewarm, and neither cold nor hot, I will spew you out of my mouth"'.

Lear Tragic hero of Shakespeare's play *King Lear*, who is cast out by his elder daughters, wanders a heath accompanied by a loyal and wise Fool, and dies after being reconciled to his youngest, faithful daughter.

Life-holder A person who holds a freehold interest in a property for the duration of his life (in *The Woodlanders* Old South has an ordinary life interest in his property. Giles Winterborne has an interest in his cottage only for the duration of South's life).

Lyric Short song-like poem in stanzas, usually expressing writer's or singer's own thoughts and sentiments.

Malign Injurious, malevolent, malignant, or ill-intent.

Medieval Of the Middle Ages (5th – 15th centuries)

Meliorism Doctrine that the world may be made better by human effort.

Melodrama Sensational dramatic piece with crude appeals to emotions and, usually, a happy ending; often dramatizing a conflict of Evil personified in the villain and extraordinary Good, personified in the hero or heroine. In the nineteenth century often a play with songs interspersed and orchestral music accompanying the action.

Metaphor Application of name of descriptive term or phrase to an object to which it is not literally applicable.

Metre Any form of poetic rhythm, determined by

character and number of poetic feet.

Narrative A tale, story, recital of facts.

Nonconformist One who does not conform to doctrine or discipline of an established Church, especially a member of a sect dissenting from the Anglican Church.

Ogee (architecture) Moulding showing in section a double continuous curve, concave below, passing into convex above, forming an S-shape. *Ogee arch* an arch with two ogee curves meeting at the apex.

Parasitic From parasite – animal or plant living in or on another and drawing nutriment directly from it; figuratively, a self-seeking hanger-on.

Pastoral Portraying country life. Originally a kind of classical poetry presenting the lives and loves of shepherds and shepherdesses.

Peripatetic Going from place to place in one's business; itinerant.

Pessimist From *pessimism* – tendency to look at the worst aspect of things or to expect bad results; doctrine that this world is the worst possible, or that all things tend to evil.

Philology Science of language.

Platonic Of Plato, the Greek philosopher (d. 347 B.C.) or his doctrines; confined to words or theory, not leading to action, harmless (platonic love – purely spiritual love).

Positivism Philosophical system of Auguste Comte, recognizing only positive facts and observable phenomena, and rejecting metaphysics and theism.

Predatory Preying naturally on others.

Prosaic Like prose; lacking poetic beauty, unromantic, commonplace, dull.

Retrospect Regard or reference to past time or events.

Romance Story of love and chivalric adventure, in prose or verse, popular during the later Middle Ages. Later prose tale with scene and incidents remote from everyday life.

Ruskin, John (1819 – 1900) Victorian writer on painting and architecture, also deeply interested in social problems. His important works include *Modern Painters* (1843 – 60), *The Seven Lamps of Architecture* (1849), *The Stones of Venice* (1851 – 3) *Unto This Last* (1862), *Sesame and Lilies* (1868).

Sanguinary Accompanied by or delighting in bloodshed; bloody.

Sapphic Verse stanza of four lines using a metre derived from the Greek poet Sappho. There are eleven syllables in each of the first three lines and five in the fourth.

Serial Issued in instalments. Of publication, appearing in successive parts published at regular intervals. In the nineteenth century serial publication in monthly or, later, weekly journals or in separately published parts was a popular form. Books published this way were subsequently issued complete in volume form.

Simile An expressed comparison between two unlike objects, usually using *like* or *as*.

Sinister Of evil omen, suggestive of evil, wicked.

Spandrel (architecture) Space between shoulder of an arch, and surrounding rectangular moulding or framework, or between shoulders of adjoining arches and moulding above.

Spontaneity From spontaneous – acting, done without external cause; involuntary; growing naturally without cultivation; automatic; gracefully natural and unconstrained.

Stereotype Unduly fixed mental impression.

Tragedy Drama in prose or verse of elevated theme and diction, with unhappy events or ending.

Transom (architecture) Horizontal bar of wood or stone across window or top of door.

Virgilian Of, or in the style of, the Roman poet Virgil (d. 19 B.C.). Virgil was the most famous classical writer of pastorals.

Further Information

Hardy's birthplace and 'Max Gate' are not open to the public. The birthplace may be viewed by appointment only.

Dorset County Museum, Dorchester, has an excellent schools service. Pamphlet guides to sites in the novels are published and are very good value. The museum houses a reconstruction of Hardy's study as well as exhibits of the period.

List of Dates

1840	1 June: Hardy born at Higher Bockhampton.
1848	Attended village school at Bockhampton.
1849	Moved to school at Dorchester.
1856-61	Articled to architect John Hicks of Dorchester. Continued classical studies; began to write verse.
1862-7	Worked for architect Arthur Blomfeld in London. Frequented theatres, art museums and exhibitions. 1865 - first published article 'How I built Myself a House'.
1867-70	Returned to Dorset; employed by Hicks on church restoration.
1868	Completed first novel, 'The Poor Man and the Lady' – never published.
1870	Met Emma Gifford while working on St. Juliot Church in Cornwall.
1871	Published *Desperate Remedies*.
1873	Invited by Leslie Stephen to write a serial for *The Cornhill*. Responded with *Far from the Madding Crowd*.
1874	Married Emma; moved to Surbiton.
1876-8	Lived at Sturminster Newton; wrote *The Return of the Native*.

1878	Lived in London.
1881	Moved to Wimborne Minster.
1883	Moved to Dorchester.
1885	Moved to 'Max Gate', the house he designed, where he lived for the rest of his life, making annual visits to London.
1888-91	Wrote and published short stories.
1891	Publication of *Tess of the d'Urbervilles*.
1892	Hardy's father died.
1896	*Jude the Obscure* published; like the reception of *Tess*, much of the response to this novel was hostile.
1897-8	Wrote and revised poems for first collection, *Wessex Poems*.
1902	Began *The Dynasts*.
1904	Hardy's mother died.
1910	Awarded the Order of Merit.
1912	Emma Hardy died.
1913	Wrote poems about Emma ('Poems 1912-13')
1914-28	Continued to write and publish poetry. Worked on *The Life of Thomas Hardy*, supposedly written by Florence.
1928	Hardy died 11 January. His ashes buried in Westminster Abbey; his heart buried in Stansford churchyard.

Further Reading

Hardy's works

The most useful collection of Hardy's novels is the New Wessex Edition of the Novels, general editor P.N. Furbank, published in 14 volumes by Macmillan (1975-76) (also available in Macmillan paperbacks). The individual novels have good introductions by a variety of well-known modern Hardy critics.

Penguin English Library also provides paperback editions, and the growing number of Hardy novels available in World's Classics paperbacks are very well edited.

Novels	Serialized
Desperate Remedies (1871)	
Under the Greenwood Tree (1872)	
A Pair of Blue Eyes (1873)	*Tinsley's Magazine* September 1872–July 1873
Far from the Madding Crowd (1874)	*Cornhill* January–December 1874
The Hand of Ethelberta (1876)	*Cornhill* July 1875–May 1876
The Return of the Native (1878)	*Belgravia* January–December 1878
The Trumpet-Major (1880)	*Good Words* January–December 1880
A Laodicean (1881)	*Harper's New Monthly Magazine* December 1880–December 1881
Two on a Tower (1882)	*Atlantic Monthly* May–December 1882
The Mayor of Casterbridge (1886)	*Graphic* January–May 1886
The Woodlanders (1887)	*Macmillan's* May 1886–April 1887

Tess of the d'Urbervilles (1891)	*Graphic* July–December 1891
Jude the Obscure (1895)	*Harper's New Monthly Magazine* December 1894–November 1895
The Well-Beloved (1897)	(as *The Pursuit of the Well-Beloved*) *Illustrated London News* October–December 1892

Stories

The New Wessex Edition of the Stories, ed. F.B. Pinion (Macmillan, 1977) provides the best collection of Hardy's short stories. It includes:

Wessex Tales (1888)
A Group of Noble Dames (1891)
Life's Little Ironies (1894)
A Changed Man (1913)
Old Mrs. Chundle and Other Stories, with The Famous Tragedy of the Queen of Cornwall

Stories are also available in Penguin English Library.

Poetry

Hardy's major volumes of poetry appeared as follows:

Wessex Poems (1898)
Poems of the Past and of the Present (1902)
The Dynasts (1903,1905,1908)
Time's Laughingstocks (1909)
Satires of Circumstance (1914)
Moments of Vision (1917)
Human Shows (1925)
Winter Words (1928)

Complete editions are:

GIBSON, J.(ed.) *The Complete Poems of Thomas Hardy* (Macmillan, 1976)
HYNES, S.(ed.) *The Complete Poems of Thomas Hardy* 3 vols (OUP, 1982-5)
OREL, H. (ed.) *The Dynasts* (1978)

The best selection for students is:

HYNES, S.(ed.) *Thomas Hardy* (Oxford Authors paperback)

Miscellaneous
BJORK, L. (ed.) The Literary Notebooks of Thomas Hardy
    2 vols (Macmillan, 1985)
COLEMAN, T. (ed.) *An Indiscretion in the Life of an Heiress* (a
    fragment of *The Poor Man and the Lady*, 1867, adapted and
    renamed) (London, 1976)
HARDY, FLORENCE E. *The Early Life of Thomas Hardy*
    1840-1891 (1928)
HARDY, FLORENCE E. *The Later Years of Thomas Hardy*
    (1930), reprinted as *The Life of Thomas Hardy* (Macmillan,
    1962)
HARDY, THOMAS *Our Adventures at West Poley* A serial
    story for boys (Puffin Books, 1983)
MILLGATE, M. (ed.) *The Life and Work of Thomas Hardy* by
Thomas Hardy (Macmillan, 1984.) (A new edition of the
    Early Life and *Later Years* by Florence Hardy)
OREL, H. (ed.) *Thomas Hardy's Personal Writings*
    (Macmillan, 1967)
PURDY, R.L. & M. MILLGATE (eds) *Collected Letters of
    Thomas Hardy* 5 vols, (1978-1985)

Biography
The Early Life of Thomas Hardy and *The Later Years of Thomas
    Hardy* (see above)
GITTINGS, R. *Young Thomas Hardy* (Heinemann, 1975)
GITTINGS, R. *The Older Hardy* (Heinemnn, 1978)
HARDY, EMMA *Some Recollections* (Oxford, 1961)
MILLGATE, M. *Thomas Hardy: A Biography* (OUP, 1982)

Writings about Hardy

This is a selected list of useful critical and biographical works about Hardy. It does not include studies of individual works. Bibliographies in these critical books will provide the student with further references to the many excellent articles on Hardy's fiction. Bibliographies in World's Classics editions are also very helpful. For a full bibliography of criticism, see: GERBER, H.E. & E.W. DAVIS (eds) *Thomas Hardy: An Annotated Bibliography of Writings About Him* (Illinois, 1973)

BAILEY, J.O. *The Poetry of Thomas Hardy* (Chapel Hill, 1970)

BAYLEY, J. *An Essay on Hardy* (Cambridge, 1978)

BOUMELHA, P. *Thomas Hardy and Women* (Harvester Press, 1982)

DAVIE, D. *Thomas Hardy and British Poetry* (1973)

GREGOR, I. *The Great Web: The Form of Hardy's Major Fiction* (1975)

LARKIN, P. 'Wanted – Good Hardy Critic' in *Required Writing* (Faber, 1984)

LAWRENCE, D.H. 'Study of Thomas Hardy' in *Phoenix: The Posthumous Papers of D.H. Lawrence* E.D. MacDonald (ed.) (1936, reprinted 1961)

MILLER, J.H. *Thomas Hardy: Distance and Desire* (1970)

MILLGATE, M. *Thomas Hardy: His Career as a Novelist* (1971)

PINION, F.B. *A Hardy Companion: A Guide to the Works of Thomas Hardy and their Background*

WILLIAMS, M. *Thomas Hardy and Rural England* (1972)

Index

Picture acknowledgements

The author and publishers would like to thank the following for allowing their illustrations to be reproduced in this book: Chapel Studios 76; acknowledgement to the Trustees of the Thomas Hardy Memorial Collection in the Dorset County Museum, Dorchester, Dorset 7, 8, 9, 10, 12, 14-15, 16, 17, 18, 19, 20, 23, 25, 27, 28, 29, 30, 32, 33, 34, 35, 37, 38, 40, 41, 43, 45, 46, 49, 51, 52, 54, 66, 67, 68, 69, 70, 71, 77, 79, 80, 92, 93, 95: the Mary Evans Picture Library 78, 88; Roger Halls 15 (bottom), 31, 48, 50, 72, 73, 75, 101; the Billie Love Collection 83, 87; National Film Archive 53, 55, 57, 58, 60, 63, 89; Ronald Sheridan's Photolibrary 22, 81, 84, 85, 86.